SNACK TIME!

Written by Barenaked Ladies

Illustrated by Kevin Hearn

Written By Barenaked Ladies
Illustrations by Kevin Hearn
Book Design by John Rummen and Christie Little @ Artwerks Design
©2008 Desperation Records

Published by Desperation Records.
Administered by Nettwerk Music Group,
1650 W. 2nd Ave., Vancouver, BC Canada v6j 4r3

Library and Archives Canada Cataloguing in Publication

Snacktime / by Barenaked Ladies ; illustrations by Kevin Hearn.
ISBN 978-1-894160-10-0

1. Children's songs, English--Canada--Texts. 2. Picture books for children.
3. Popular music--Canada--Texts. I. Hearn, Kevin II. Barenaked Ladies (Musical group)

M1997.S669 2008   j782.42'0268'083   C2008-901863-X
Printed in Canada.

789

123 and 4 more makes 7
and 6 is afraid of 7...
cause 7 ate 9!

Nine was minding his business
talking to 10 about Gordy Howe's clothes
why 7 ate 9, nobody knows

1 2 3 **4** 5 **6** 7 8 **10**
What about 9?

7 ate 9!

Oh the cat'll have to live with eight lives now
Ronaldo will have to make do
Ever since seven ate nine it seems
I've got an extra finger an extra toe too

7 ate 9!

once upon a time in our solar system
We couldn't make do without 9
But Pluto's not a planet now, so 8'll do fine

Oh, the cat'll have to do with 8 lives now
And the Chinese will be out of luck
And vampires will have to think of some other method
cause without their K-9s,
how will they suck?

7 ate 9!

1 2 **3** **4** 5 **6** 7 **8** **10**
What about 9?

7 ate 9!

The Ninjas

I woke up this morning and everything was different
Something was strange in the air
I woke up this morning and everything was different
I knew that The Ninjas had been there

I looked all around my bedroom
Underneath the dresser
Behind the bed, but nothing could be found
There was nothing left behind them
No way that I could find them
No fingerprints or crumbs on the ground.

The Ninjas are deadly and silent
They're also unspeakably violent
They speak Japanese; do whatever they please,
And sometimes they vacation in Ireland.

The Ninjas are deadly and silent
They're also unspeakably violent
They speak Japanese; do whatever they please,
And if you tear off their masks, they'll be smiling.

Pollywog in a Bog

In the puddle by the trail it flips its tiny tail
Just like a great big whale but smaller than a snail

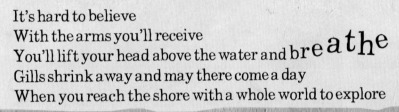

It's a Pollywog in a bog
Swims under soggy logs
One day he'll be a frog
Pollywog in a bog

Overhead a cedar tree gives the shade he needs
Munching while he feeds on lily pads and weeds

Knows not where he's from
Or how his life had begun
He's not the only one
And soon he'll breathe through lungs

It's hard to believe
With the arms you'll receive
You'll lift your head above the water and breathe
Gills shrink away and may there come a day
When you reach the shore with a whole world to explore

Ribbit Ribbit a tadpole exhibit
It's a transformation no one can inhibit
Amphibian change may seem strange
Take them gills and the tail and they all rearrange

Out come the legs for the Jump! Jump! Hop to the top of the Stump! Stump!
Out come the legs for the Jump! Jump! Hop to the top of the Stump! Stump!

Where the mud is deep frost will soon creep
And without a peep a frog is fast asleep

It was a Pollywog in a bog
Swam under soggy logs
In the morning fog
Pollywog in a bog

Raisins

Raisins come from Grapes
People come from Apes
I come from Canada
I came in first place
In a non existent race
To rebuild the Parthenon

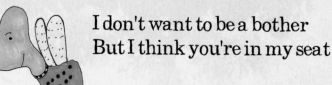

The Parthenon's in Greece
Or was it in Grease 2
I can't keep my movies straight
When I make mistakes
I use a lot of salt
Cause salt makes m'steaks taste great

I don't want to be a bother
But I think the phone's for you

I've got orange pants
I wear them when I dance
But I don't get out that much
You are just too loud
I passed you in a crowd
Thank you and keep in touch

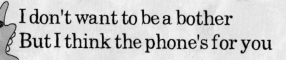

I don't speak Chinese
Not even words like "please"
"Thank you", or "how are you"
But I can parle Francais
I parled a bit today
It seemed like the thing to do

I don't want to be a bother
But I think you're in my seat

Eraser

Eraser!
Eraser!

Eraser!

I draw it with a pencil!
Because it's just a stencil.
And if I do retry it well then I can't deny it.
I'm gonna need my little eraser.

Eraser!
Eraser. Eraser
Eraser!
Eraser. Eraser

Eraser!

I might have to redo it.
I might have to work through it.
But I try not to chew it.
Cause I just shouldn't do it.
Cause I might need my little eraser.

If I wrote you a letter, but I made an error, I could fix it
And make it better.

If I make an error I can always make it better with my eraser.

ERASER! ERASER! ERASER!

Eraser!
Eraser. Eraser.

Eraser!

Eraser. Eraser.

Eraser!

Eraser. Eraser.

Eraser!

I Can Sing

I can Sing!
I can sing! I can sing better.
I can knit a scarf but you can't knit a sweater.
When I'm underwater, I couldn't be wetter.
Never go swimmin'
in a mohair sweater.

I can dance I can dance
I can dance f a s t e r
I tried to keep up but it was a disaster.
One more move and I'm gonna be
the master!
So crank it up loud on the ghetto blaster

I can eat I can eat I can eat more
And when it's not fresh from the local store
There's a little town in Labrador
Where she sells seashells
by the shoe store

I can speak I can speak
I can speak quicker

Imagine I made a new way to make
everyone currently frowning snicker!

And on the guitar he could be a little slicker

But Jimmy always said I was a good flatpicker

Dive down
Into the cool green water
Swim around
By the fish and otters

Louis Loon
Louis Loon

Flap your wings
You're picking up speed
Soon you'll spring
High above the trees

Louis Loon

June the beaver
Below you'll leave her

Gnawing on sticks
With another dam to fix

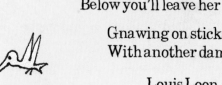

Louis Loon

She hears your song
Echoing over lakes and hills
Lonely and long
Sometimes it's high, sometimes with a trill

Where ever you are
You are admired from a far
But just around the bend
You can always call your friends
Call your friends

Splash Splash
Come on in and land
In a flash
You're under water again

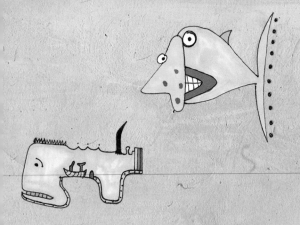

Looking to see
When you surface where you'll be

Won't you stay?
Your friends want to play

Won't you stay?
Your friends want to play

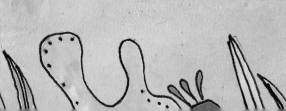

THAT WAS THE FINAL MOVEMENT OF
Anton Corbijn's

FOOD PARTY

Featuring
ED SHAUGHNESSY ON CLAVES

NEXT UP ON
RADIO C-A-K-E

Barenaked Ladies
With
THE CANADIAN SNACKTIME
TRILOGY

The Canadian Snacktime Trilogy

SNACK TIME

I wake up in the morning. I go to sleep at night,

but a day without snack time, that just isn't right.

Oh snack time. Oh Snack time.

How I love the vision of people everywhere

in harmony together and each one has their share.

Oh snack time. Oh Snack time.

Snack time. Snack time. Talkin' 'bout snack time.

Snack time. Snack time. Oh snack time.

Snack time. Snack time. Oh Snack time.

POPCORN

Mama put the popcorn kernels in the pot.

She turned up the heat now the pot is getting hot.

And then those popcorn kernels start to pop,

pop   pop

pop   pop ...POPCORN!

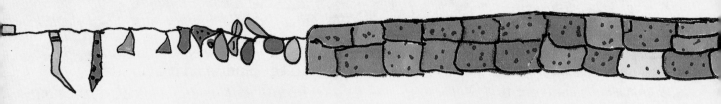

VEGETABLE TOWN

The houses are built with leafy lettuce.

The light posts are all rubbery asparagus, in Vegetable Town.

The roads are paved with sautéed onions.

Community Hall is a hollow pumpkin, in Vegetable Town.

Won't you walk me down to Vegetable Town?

Won't you walk me down to Vegetable Town?

Where we can ride the zucchini subway,

or watch the carrot planes land on the runway.

In Vegetable Town. In Vegetable Town.

Won't you walk me down to Vegetable Town?

Won't you walk me down to Vegetable Town?

To Vegetable Town. To Vegetable Town.

Won't you walk me down to Vegetable Town?

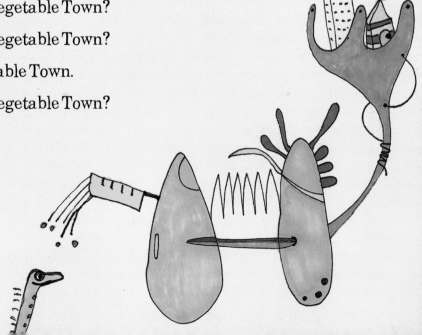

DRAWING!

There's a blueberry
pancake flying in the sky
I can see it. I can see it.

There's a castle
in the cloud and it's floating
on by can you see it? Can you see it?

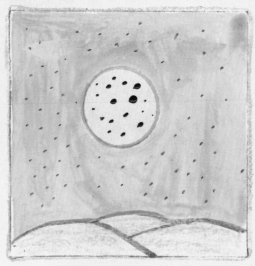 

With my imagination I can see it! With my pencil crayons I can draw it!
On a piece of paper I can show it to you. I can show it to you.

There's a purple hippopotamus
riding on a bike I can see it.
I can see it.

There's a spaceship
over my house at night
I just know it. I just know it.

With my imagination I can see it! With my pencil crayons I can draw it!
On a piece of paper I can show it to you! I can show it to you.
Draw, Draw, Drawing. Na na na na na. Draw, Draw, Drawing. Na na na na na.
My imagination. My imagination. My pencil crayons. My imagination.

Humungous Tree

I'm gonna plant this seed, this little tiny seed,
and it is gonna grow into a giant tree.
A gigantic tree. A ginormous tree.
A humungous tree for all the world to see..

You've gotta love the trees,
they even help us breathe.
They give us oxygen.
They give us scenery.
When I see a healthy trunk it makes me want to jump.
But I feel the opposite when I see a stump.

Help me plant this seed, this little tiny seed.
And let us watch it grow into a giant tree.
One gigantic tree here for you and me.
For our children's children's children's
children's children to see.

My Big Sister

I like my big sister.
But I don't want to wear her coat.
It may be black
It may fit perfect
But you and I both know it's a girl's coat

Now I can handle some hand me downs
But shirts and sandals are out of bounds
Balls and games and such I don't mind
But a coat is over the line

ALLERGIES

ALLERGIES

ALLERGIC TO CATS   ALLERGIC TO BEES
ALLERGIC TO DUST   ALLERGIC TO TREES
ALLERGIC TO MOLD   ALLERGIC TO WEEDS

MY LITTLE BROTHER IS ALLERGIC TO MEAT
MY FRIENDS MOTHER IS ALLERGIC TO WHEAT
ALLERGIC TO MEAT?   ALLERGIC TO WHEAT?
IT'S GOTTA BE TRICKY FINDING SOMETHING TO EAT!

ALLERGIES

ALLERGIC TO DOGS   ALLERGIC TO FROGS
ALLERGIC TO NUTS   I HATE THEIR GUTS
ALLERGIC TO SMOKE   IT MAKES ME CHOKE
ALLERGIC TO SHRIMP   I BLOW UP LIKE A BLIMP

I GET ALL ITCHY AND I START TO WHEEZE
EVEN IF I SEE A SLICE OF CHEESE
A SLICE OF CHEESE?   I START TO WHEEZE
HANG ON FELLAS I'M ABOUT TO SNEEZE
AHH, AHHH, AHHHH – CHOO!!

ALLERGIES   ALLERGIES

ALLERGIC TO DOGS   ALLERGIC TO FROGS
ALLERGIC TO EGGS   ALLERGIC TO LEGS
ALLERGIC TO HEADS   ALLERGIC TO BEDS
ALLERGIC TO BARK   IT MAKES ME SNARK
ALLERGIC TO FACE   ALLERGIC TO BASS
ALLERGIC TO GUITARS   ALLERGIC TO THE STARS
ALLERGIC TO YOU   ALLERGIC TO ME
ALLERGIC TO BIRDS   ALLERGIC TO BEES

AAAAAAAGGGGGGGGHHHHHHHHH!!!!!!!!!!

I Don't Like

I can eat pork 'til the cows come home
And cheese like it's going out of style
I like just about every type of vegetable
I like raisins, and nuts, and seeds, and olives,
And pickles, and fruit, and beef, and bread,
But I don't like... salmon.

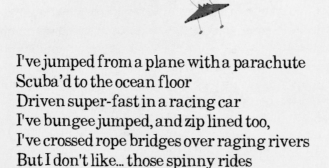

I've jumped from a plane with a parachute
Scuba'd to the ocean floor
Driven super-fast in a racing car
I've bungee jumped, and zip lined too,
I've crossed rope bridges over raging rivers
But I don't like... those spinny rides

I can fly my very own aeroplane
And I've been to the top of mountains
I've been to the top of the CN Tower
I can work on a ladder, I can climb a tree
I can look out the window of a really tall building
But if I stand close to the edge of a railing, or up on a roof or something I realize
I don't like... heights so much

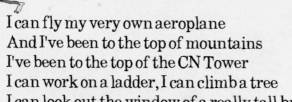

What A Wild Tune

Last night I heard the wolves.
Last night I heard the wolves.
Last night I heard the wolves they were howling at the moon.
Howling at the moon.
Howling at the moon. What a wild tune they were howling at the moon.

Last night I heard the breeze.
Last night I heard the breeze.
Last night I heard the breeze it was singing through the trees.

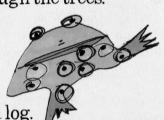

Then I heard some frogs.
Then I heard some frogs.
Then I heard some frogs they were croaking on a log.

There's music in the air.
There's music in the air.
There's music in the air and the air is everywhere.

Last night I heard the wolves.
Last night I heard the wolves.
Last night I heard the wolves they were howling at the moon.
Howling at the moon.

Bad Day

I'm having a bad day

There's nothing you can do or say To help me through this bad day

I think I'll just stay in my room They didn't need to say That they didn't want to play

I could have guessed it anyway And that's why I'm here in my room

Seems like I'm the only one Who's not outside and having fun

I wish this day had never begun

I think I'll just stay in my room Sometimes I want to run and hide

Today I want to stay inside Tell my bike to take itself for a ride

I'm staying in today See the toys lying on the floor

I don't want them anymore Think I'll sell them back to the store

Or give them all away Seems like I'm the only one

Who's not outside and having fun I wish this day had never begun

I think I'll just stay in my room I don't need hugs and I don't want food

I want to stay here in this lonely mood I don't care if people think I'm rude

I wish they would all go away Dad comes in and tells me with a kiss

That everyone has days like this He brought my dinner,

said that I was missed I think I'll be okay

I know I'm not the only one To stay inside and watch the fun

Thanks a lot, that helped a ton Tomorrow's going to be a better day

Things

There are things that make me

You are not one of them

There are things that make me

 sad

But you are not one of them

There are things that make me

You seem to be all of them

Curious

If I climb a Tree just to see what I see
Does that make me curious?
If I make a point of just cruising a joint
Would that make me curious?
And if it's profound this just lookin' around
Well then gee whiz
Don't call me crazy
Never been Lazy
Curious it is

A touch of excess with a little finesse
Is simply Luxurious
And if I confess to makin' this mess
Would that make you furious
But after a while you'll be crackin' a smile
And that's when we'll see
If I may submit you'll have to admit
You're curious like me

They say that curiosity was responsible
For the unfortunate demise of the cat
But with 8 more lives to investigate
What kind of a deal is that? Not Bad

A furious sun can make for serious fun
So we wont let that worry us
Cause the fun is outdone by a barrel of one
If that one's the furriest
If curious mean that you trade your routines
For something free
The freedom you feel's the whole point of the deal so
Curious I'll be

Curiouser, and curiouser Sir
Curious
Curious like
Curious like me

There's a word for that
But I don't seem to know it
Sometimes I grow a moustache just so I don't have to show it
The word for that
That someone, somewhere chose
For that little dented skin between my upper lip and nose

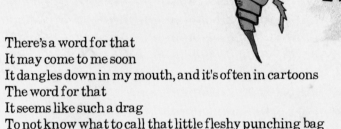

A Word For That

There's a word for that
What does it start with?
A word for that
I'd sound so smart if I only knew
The word for that
Perhaps you do?

There's a word for that
It may come to me soon
It dangles down in my mouth, and it's often in cartoons
The word for that
It seems like such a drag
To not know what to call that little fleshy punching bag

There's a word for that
What does it start with?
A word for that
I'd sound so smart if I only knew
The word for that
Perhaps you do?

Philtrum, Uvula and Frenulum!....
What's the big deal??

There's a word for that
It's on the tip of my tongue
Well actually underneath it, and has been since I was young
The word for that
Although I wouldn't quote
It likely stops my tongue from disappearing down my throat

There's a word for that
What does it start with?
A word for that
I'd sound so smart if I only knew
The word for that
Perhaps you do?
What does it start with?
The word for that
I'd sound so smart if I only knew
The word for that

Wishing

I wish I could speak with my dog
I wish I could speak with my dog
I wish I could speak with my dog
Cause right now it's just a monologue

I wish I could walk on a cloud
I wish I could walk on a cloud
I wish I could walk on a cloud
I sure wish Cloud walkin' was aloud

I wish every wish would come true
I wish every wish would come true
I wish every wish would come true
Cause it sure feels good when they do

Crazy ABCs

A is for Aisle

B is for Bdellium

C is for Czar, and if you see him would you mind telling him??

D is fo Djinn

E for Euphrates

F is for Fohn, but not like when I call the ladies

G is for Gnarly

I for Irk

H is for Hour

J for Jalapeno, good in either corn or flour... tortillas.

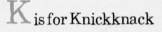

K is for Knickknack

L is or llama

M for Mnemonic

N is for Ngomo

O is for Ouija Board

P is for Pneumonia, Pterodactyl, and Psychosis

Q is for Qat

R is for RGyle.

S is for Saar, a lovely german river

T for Tsunami, a wave that makes me quiver

U is for Urn, and not like earning money

V for Vraisemblance from french and therefore sort of funny

W for Wren, Wrinkly and Who

X is for Xi'an, an ancient Chinese city, True

Y is for Yperite, a very nasty gas

Z is the final letter, and by final I mean last

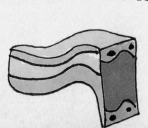

Here Come The Geese

Look up in the sky, they said on the radio station.
They're up quite high, flying in a V formation.

Here come the geese!
Here come the geese!

Now they're on the lawns, the patios and ponds, on the sidewalks,
on the rooftops, on the hillside, on the playground slide, in the shadows,
the parking lots, the meadows, the fences and ledges,
benches and hedges, in the schoolyard, on the boulevard,
in the high school halls, in the shopping malls.
Watch under your feet, they said on the radio station.

Here come the geese!

Flying in a V formation.

Written by ...

Ed

Tyler

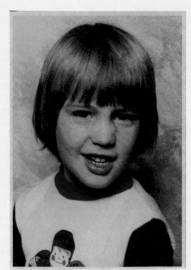

Steven

and Jackson

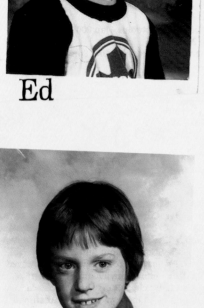

Kevin

Jim